Millie:
Our One in a
Million

Millie: Our One in a Million

ISBN: 978-1-911227-19-9
First edition: July 2019

Credits
Editor: Nicci Robinson
Production design: Global Wordsmiths
Cover design by Global Wordsmiths

Millie: Our One In A Million

GRENVILLE MORLEY

2019

Acknowledgments

First of all, I want to thank Ian and Tara who initially assisted me get our story into print with help on the computer and typing up the first couple of chapters. Secondly, I'd like to thank my sister-in-law, Karen, for typing the first draft of the story from my written notes.

Many thanks to Nicci Robinson from Global Wordsmiths, a lovely young lady who was introduced to us by our son, Ian, after meeting her at Awsworth School. Nicci became my editor and has been so professional in her understanding of my wanting to share Millie's story.

My thanks also go to Polly Thomas at the ATP School for Dogs. Without this lady, Millie would definitely have had something missing from her life. What a brilliant experience for us to have trained our dog with someone so devoted to helping owners give their dogs a wonderful life. Gloria Morgan of Dayglo Books was so supportive when we showed her the first draft of my story. She pointed the way to go and gave me advice, for which I'm very grateful.

Thank you to all the dogs and their owners at the APT Training classes who helped to provide the perfect atmosphere for all our happy dogs to develop and thrive.

Thank you to Ann at Lawrence Veterinary Surgery Eastwood and all at Willows Veterinary Centre Solihull for their expertise and especially for the kindness they showed to Millie.

Many thanks to our sons, their wives and partners, and our wonderful grandchildren who were always there to enrich Millie's family life.

Dedication

To my dear wife, Elaine; my right arm.
Thank you will never be enough to say how wonderful you've been in helping me put this book together to tell others of the marvellous time we had with our pet, Millie.

None of it would have been possible without you.

Foreword

Hello Reader,

You are privileged because you're about to read a heartwarming story about Millie, a corgi who was definitely One in a Million.

I was extremely fortunate to meet Grenville and Elaine when they brought Millie to my training school and started on my Puppy/Beginner level. Apparently my first comment to them, which I can't remember but Grenville does was, "Oh! You've got one of those."

Corgis are often difficult to train but not so with Millie. Grenville took on board with enormous enthusiasm everything he was shown, and Millie started to show improvements far beyond what I could ever have hoped for.

Over the years Millie gradually climbed through my various levels of training until she worked at the top level of Platiplus2, a level not many owners and their dogs ever accomplished. She thoroughly enjoyed my extra classes at agility, she performed at our fete demonstrations, and she did loads of fundraising.

A class with Millie and Grenville in it was always a class of laughter. My life has been enriched by knowing this happy, loving family, and I hope that by reading this book, yours will be too.

Polly Thomas,
APT School for Dogs

A Few More Words

I had the great pleasure of getting to know Millie when I took my own dog to the same obedience training class. I know how hard my dog and I worked to achieve our bronze, silver, and gold awards, but we never came within sight of the clever tricks that Millie learned to do.

Grenville and Elaine put in hours and hours of dedication to teach Millie the many intricate and amusing routines she mastered. We would gasp in amazement as she went through her paces, doing exactly as she was told and never putting a paw out of place.

I know from experience that achievement at that level is only attained through hours and hours of practice. But when you love a dog as much as Millie was loved, every minute of that practice is a pleasure. And Millie only wanted to please—her little tail never stopped wagging.

I hope you will enjoy reading about this beautiful, clever, and happy dog as much as I enjoyed knowing her.

Gloria Morgan,
Dayglo Books Ltd

Introduction

Come with my wife, Elaine, and I on a very special journey with our pet, a Welsh Pembrokeshire corgi named Millie.

A dog can be a true friend; always there for you day after day no matter what. So comforting in times of sadness or stress. Unconditional love always reciprocated. Our first corgi we named Honey. She was fifteen years old when we lost her through illness. The reason we had Honey in the first place was because for about three months before, we had looked after our mum's dog, a Pembrokeshire corgi named Trixie, after Mum had a hip replacement. When Mum recovered from her operation, Trixie went back home with her.

Straight away we felt a little spirit was missing from our house, especially when the key was turned, and we opened the door—there was no usual welcome! We found that we certainly needed a pet of our own, and we had many wonderful years with Honey.

A year after we lost Honey, along came Millie. For some reason we always thought that we knew best on how to train and look after Honey, though we would occasionally take advice from other dog owners. Elaine had dogs in her family since childhood, including corgis, and had a lot of experience with dogs in general, but I only had cats until my early teens. I will always remember Elaine's family dog, George. He was a Rhodesian ridgeback—only a slight difference, you could say! A wonderful, gentle, powerful animal he was! Hence, Elaine had lots of training tips to help our corgis. Honey was a happy, friendly dog who could do a lot of party tricks, and she was so well behaved. Only now do we know how much she would have enjoyed going to training classes and blossomed even more.

In this book, we show how we trained Millie in the hope that it helps you to understand how training your dog properly can be really fulfilling to both you and your pet: your "One in a Million!"

Contents

An Ending Becomes A New Beginning

We remember driving home that day from the vets in Nottingham after saying goodbye to our lovely pet, Honey. We'd told her she had always been a good girl, and we loved her dearly.

She was fifteen years old when she was finally taken from us with acute kidney failure. The previous day we had telephoned Davison's Vets, and they said it would be best to take Honey in to see them straight away. After arriving with Honey, we booked in and sat down in the waiting area with her laying across both our laps. The vet came to us, carefully lifted her, and carried her into the surgery. He told us she needed urgent attention, that they would make her comfortable and do everything they could. As he walked away with her, she had her head over his shoulder and she was looking at us and we understood her look of "Good-bye, Mum and Dad." *Goodnight, little one*. The vet called us the next morning to say that she was very sick. She'd stayed in there overnight, and we already felt that her chances of recovery were slim. He said that we could come and stay with her if we liked...before it was "time."

As soon as we saw her when she was brought into the room, we knew it was that dreadful "time" to say a final good-bye to her. Honey, our adorable

Pembrokeshire corgi, was gone. What a loving and playful dog she had been. A member of our family for fifteen years.

Going home, Elaine and I said there was no way we could go through that heartache again. We had lost such a dear little friend.

The first few days after we lost Honey we went through the motions of clearing up her mats, playthings, and bowls etc. Photos and memories would, of course, stay forever.

One of her favourite play things was a smooth marbled stone with one flat side. Let me explain where the stone came from.

One summer's evening when Honey was a pup, we were walking on a footpath at the side of a cornfield in Watnall when suddenly she just scampered off into the corn.

"Honey," we shouted. "Come out of there!"

We could see the tops of the corn moving where she was running and assumed she was chasing a mouse or something larger! The corn stopped moving, and we thought she had caught whatever it was she was after. We went in to see what she was doing. Guess what? She had her nose on a stone, and she'd been pushing it along the ground with her nose! Why? We'll never know, but she didn't want to leave it, so I picked it up and took it home. We gave it a good wash and even polished it up. It soon proved to be one of her favourite playthings. And over the years most of our family and friends would say to her "Honey, where's your stone?" She would find it and push it with her nose along the carpet like it was on ice, right up to your feet! You just know that we still have that stone which is simply priceless.

Honey was such a loss, and as we've said before we didn't think we could go through that again. That was it, or so we thought…

At the time, we had a busy motor body repair business, and over the next few months important business issues such as deadlines on vehicle repairs and generally having a lot to do in our busy workshop seemed to help heal the loss of our pet. Keeping busy usually helps at heart-breaking times, and we really found it to be the case.

Love at First Sight

Eleven months later I was examining a damaged car when Elaine came out of the office and said that she had something to show me. At first, I thought that it was probably a go-ahead from an insurance company to complete some repairs.

"Look here," she said and pointed to the screen on the desk.

What I saw was completely unexpected: thirteen corgi pups on the screen. Where did all these pups come from? Apparently, Grandma and Mummy corgi had pups at the same time, hence such a beautiful bundle.

Can you imagine all those beautiful corgi puppies? But how could we possibly consider having another one after what we'd been through a year ago?

After talking about it over and over again, we came to the same conclusion. The love between Honey and ourselves was pushing us towards wanting to give another corgi a home. And so, it started all over again. Excitement wasn't the word on the morning we travelled to Wolverhampton. We'd already phoned and arranged to see the puppies at Wharrytons. We simply had to go and choose one of the pups.

On arriving at the breeders, we were met by owner, Mrs. Jameson, and she took us through to see them.

What a sight! What a wonderful sight! So many puppies; some playing and some dozing on top of each other. One puppy was multi-coloured with a tail that was mostly black apart from a small amount of white at the tip and it was being chased around by its siblings. What fun they were having!

We were looking for a red one with a white bib front and white "boots."

"Here she is with her mum, as usual," Mrs Jameson said.

And there she was. She was slightly smaller than her brothers and sisters, and what a pretty little thing she was! Apparently, although she played a lot, most of the time she was her mum's shadow. Her mum was a beautiful colour and very friendly towards us. We were told that Millie's kennel name was Wharryton's Photo Finish. Her grandad had a gene that caused some of the puppies to have a small tail. His kennel name included the name, Kodak, hence Millie's kennel name, as she was also born with a small tail.

But this was it! Millie was to be ours in a fortnight! Two months previous, we'd purchased tickets to see the Everly Brothers in Bournemouth. So it worked out that we could make a detour on the way back from the show, to pick up our puppy.

Two weeks later, we could barely contain our excitement. We made our way up the path which had numerous corgi signs and ornamental corgis in the garden. Mrs Jameson introduced us to her husband, and then we went through to the puppies.

After the formalities of certificates and other paperwork, Millie was officially ours to look after for the rest of her life. It turns out that one of her sisters was already on her way to Australia!

We were about to leave when Mr Jameson said, "Do

you mind if I carry her to the car?"

"Of course you may," I said, thinking that our Millie was probably his favourite. After handing Millie over, I popped her onto a blanket on Elaine's lap in the front seat. Mr Jameson looked as though he was parting with a dog he'd had for years, not weeks. Clearly, he already knew how special she was.

On the way back, we took a wrong turn and that's something I'm famous for doing in my family! Millie was whining, and it started to snow! Home seemed a long way away, but we arrived safely and Millie christened our front lawn with a tiddle.

Millie soon learned that she loved the snow!

I opened the front door, and she ran straight through the hall and into the lounge. She stopped abruptly when she saw her reflection in the black glass of the video cabinet and immediately started darting around and barking at it as if to say, "My brothers and sisters are in there!"

But no, she would have to settle with her new mum and dad. And she did. Family and friends soon started to come around to see our beautiful corgi pup. She settled in with no problems, with just a little whining and an occasional bark at night. But even that didn't last long.

Millie enjoyed the outside and the garden, and she very quickly learned that outside was the place to be when she needed the toilet. Good girl! Well, a couple of weeks later, we took her on a trip to Lawrence's Vets in Eastwood for her booster vaccinations before she was to go into the big wide world. She was invited to attend a party for a little socialising with other puppies. It was a really good experience for Millie; she was given lots of freebies and a new toy—a plastic treat cube for small biscuits which she pushed around with her nose until the treat popped out. It was a fun thing that she had for years!

Buddies and Biscuits

There we were on the first trip into the fields. Millie was on her pretty new lead, so we headed up the road and over the stile. What a big world this was for her. She bounded about like a little lamb, running up and down the hills. Sometimes, she would just stop and sit at the top of the hill and look across over Nottingham as if to say, "I can see forever."

At home, Millie was like most pups; always wanting to play. When we called her, she would run toward us and dash right underneath us as we knelt down, especially when we had one of her toys behind us. The children loved it and thought it hilarious. Millie thought that everyone who came to the house had come to see her, and that never changed! About this time, if we happened to have an arm hanging out of the bed in the morning, she'd find it, and lick it and lick it until we woke. Was she telling us it was time to get up? Nope, more like, "Can I have my breakfast, please?"

Over the next few months or so, Millie made one or two friends. Next door, Sue and Jason, had a boxer dog, Cara, who greeted her new neighbour with a lovely hello that consisted of half a bark and a funny little snort! They were fast friends! She also found friends on her first walks in the fields at the back of Trough

Road in our village of Watnall. Another Sue, who lived around the corner from us, had Megan, an English springer spaniel. Megan was the first dog Millie learned to recognise in the fields when we were out walking. Up the hill she would run to meet her friend. Megan was just the dog for Millie to take a few tips on how to behave.

One morning on the same hill, we came upon Hovis, another springer spaniel, and his owner, Kathy. We were talking about how we hoped Millie would settle down just like Honey had done. Puppy training came into our conversation, and Kathy mentioned that she'd taken Hovis to a lady, Polly Thomas, who ran several classes for dog training at the APT School for Dogs.

We said that we were very interested and would love to start Millie on some puppy training. Kathy gave us the phone number for APT, and we rang Polly that day. After talking to her on the phone, we arranged to go and see what the classes were all about.

***

All makes, shapes, and sizes of dogs were there when we entered the hall. Taking time out for us, Polly came over to greet us with our six-month-old pup. She looked at Millie and said comically, "Oh! One of those!"

Well, we sat round the hall and watched how the owners and their dogs were asked to participate at times altogether or individually. Obviously, there were several dogs at different levels of training, so when each dog and their owner was asked to go out on their own to the middle of the hall, Polly instructed them on their particular level to carry out her instructions as requested. We immediately said how an environment with lots of well-behaved dogs would help Millie to be well-behaved too. There were one or two dogs not quite managing to settle, but within this environment the animals do settle eventually and really enjoy their tasks.

Good behaviour brings rewards. The dogs soon catch on to this and it spreads over to most of the animals attending the classes. We were shown how a little check tug of the lead sideways on would eventually bring your dog under control in circumstances where they misbehave, such as barking incessantly for no apparent reason. Sometimes a little spray of water on the nose from a plastic water spray bottle helps with this or with the pooch pulling on their lead and not paying attention to Mum or Dad at all! A small treat now and again didn't go amiss at this crucial time in training. Polly was always there on hand if help was needed. This was a time when we first heard Polly say, "Train their brains as often as their legs!" We found that to be very true.

You can never put in too much time in this first development stage to bond with your pet. For example, when you're making a command to your dog, we were shown how the use of your arms and hands on their own can be used to convey various instructions and to use your voice also. Different tones of voice start to have an effect on what action your dog will take. The aim of all this hard work is to make for a happy dog in most circumstances. Total trust is the key to that special bond, which is just priceless.

Millie was at the very first rung of her training ladder. We soon started to learn the key areas to build from. The first week there, we were told that we needed a proper leather lead for her and a collar tag with only a phone number and not her name, and that we should always carry a pooh bag! Slapped legs if you didn't have that bag on test day! That slip could tip the marks from a pass into a fail! We started taking Millie to training every Wednesday afternoon and the first six weeks soon went by, which was all about puppy training. Elaine carried out a lot of exercise training at home, such as heel work when walking with her on lead and teaching her to sit on command. She put in such a lot of time with Millie, and it soon started to show. After telling her to sit, Elaine would hold a treat on the bridge of her nose and say, "Millie, watch!" Immediate eye contact always had a swift reward! All these exercises were taken from the training classes…homework, if you like!

After a few weeks, Millie wasn't shifting her eyes off that treat, no matter what noise or commotion was happening around her, which always deserved a lot of praise.

Her first recall in the hall where we trained was delightful. There she was, this little corgi pup, right at the other end of the long hall. Polly had her by the lead, and we had to call her from the opposite end of the room. "Millie, come. Millie, come," was all that was required to get her to come. She'd run as fast as she could, skidding a little on the wooden floor, her ears flapping, straight up to our feet. Grabbing hold of her collar, as we'd been taught, we rewarded her with three little tit-bits one after another.

Kerb control, crossing the road, etcetera was all part of the first level, which was the APT puppy foundation course. Millie passed it quite easily, and we were so proud of her. And us! To teach an animal how to behave and most of all, for Millie to enjoy her surroundings and this big world. To be part of it!

As well as a good walk in the morning and at night, Millie went to her weekly classes, which involved five weeks training for each level of attainment, from bronze up to platinum two grade. The sixth week was test day.

This afternoon it was the real first rung up the

ladder, which was bronze. No problems at all for Millie. When Polly handed out our bronze rosette, it was just like winning at the Olympics! Millie always had a look as if to say, "Okay, where are the biccies?"

Millie's confidence grew every day, and it was lovely to see her friends in the doggy world on walks, recognising the owners (especially if they put their hand into their treat pocket!). One day we remember her running into the kitchen, all excited. Looking at her, we laughed and said, "What have you got there?" I put my hand under her mouth and said, "Give!" After she'd dropped a clothes peg into my hand, I said, "Good girl, helping to tidy up!" Hearing that, she immediately knew she should be treated to a biccie! We gave her a gravy bone biscuit, as I happened to have one handy in my pocket. That was the start of her love affair with those special treats!

Stranger Danger v Heidi the Lurcher and Friends

When walking in one of the local fields this particular afternoon, we were coming up to a man and his dog who we didn't recognise. Millie inquisitively just walked merrily towards the Staffordshire bull terrier. Don't get me wrong, we know some lovely Staffies, especially one at training classes, but Millie was about to learn about stranger danger in a shocking way. The dog made a sudden jump at her and knocked her over.

She'd never been an aggressive pup, so she simply submitted and rolled onto her back. But this didn't help. The dog attacked her and began to bite her tummy. We quickly intervened, and luckily, we were able to get the dog off her before things escalated even further. I pulled Millie up into my arms, but the dog kept jumping up after her! The owner strolled over, put his dog on its lead and just walked away. We were both aghast, although Millie wasn't injured. It's bad enough when your dog is attacked, but we couldn't help but wonder, what if Millie had been a small child? It just didn't bear thinking about! Surely this behaviour from this dog should not have gone unchecked. If I hadn't been so shocked at the time, I would've asked the man if he loved the animal he was walking with, and I would have advised him to take the time for a spot of training to help his dog to socialize with its friends in the canine world. We have a granddaughter who was traumatized by a dog that acted aggressively towards her in her local park. It took a long time for her not to be afraid of *every* dog she came across whenever she was out in a park. If someone can't recall their dog, something is wrong, and it should be kept on a lead. All it takes is a few hours of some basic training; attaining a bronze at training classes is the perfect way to address this behaviour. We never had an apology. We saw the dog several times after that incident, and it was always on a lead. Never again did it know freedom. It was very sad and not the dog's fault—it was the owner in the wrong.

Millie fitted herself in easily with our regular home life. Like most dogs, they all find their little special places to nap instead of going to their bed. Millie's favourite place was on the settee with her head on one of the arms. She also loved it in the corner of the chair; she'd lie upside down, legs up and flat out! We lost count of the number of photos we took of her in that position! Another favourite place was behind the curtains in the lounge with her back to the wall. All we could see was her paws sticking out from underneath. Snooze time!

She soon learned that the children coming around, or any time we had a party, usually meant some tasty nibbles to be had off the floor. We taught her to wait until the treat was put down, eye contact made, and a "Good girl" was said. Only then should she snap it up!

***

Two good walks every day, rain or shine, Millie

was always up for it. Around the fields and through the woods, and sometimes we would let her choose which way she wanted to go. Always eager to explore, but occasionally looking back to make sure we were right behind her. We always put her on her lead when necessary, especially where farm animals were kept in the field, and when walking by the roadside.

When we met other owners with their dogs, the animals would stand, play around a little or simply sit together. One sunny morning, Millie met a dog she had a chase around with. Heidi was a beautiful Lurcher, and it was the beginning of a wonderful friendship. What fun and games they had!

Heidi was very clever at playing cat and mouse with Millie. Every time they met, they would run around in a very wide circle and Millie would try to cut her off. But Heidi was too smart for that! She would stop on a sixpence and just lurch the opposite way. All I can say is that it resembled a rabbit chasing a greyhound. Other friends of Millie's included Dillon, a grey setter. He definitely seemed to be in a world of his own. No matter how much Millie wanted to play, he wasn't having any of it! He would just run straight past us out of nowhere and didn't want to know about playing with her. Millie always stood still and watched, quite bemused. But he didn't have an angry hair on his body; a lovely pooch.

Sometimes on a walk we would meet up with our neighbours, Jane and Graham, and their springer spaniel, Henry. He loved his walks up the fields, even though his sight failed him in his later years. Millie always showed her respect for him, just naturally like she did with Doug and Susan's cairn terrier, Katie. We often used to have a chat when we met up walking the dogs. The dogs were very patient at these meetings as Doug and I would ramble on about happenings and people in the motor trade in the sixties and seventies. We always had a good laugh! Susan and Doug once told us how Katie had to have one eye removed early on in her life and then lost the other one a year later. But the little dog soldiered on and showed everyone how resilient she was. No, you don't need eyes to love! And she showed that for many a year. They told us how she always knew where she was and who they were talking to by her actions. What a wonderful, brave little dog she was.

There was Carolyn and her Labrador, Max, and Heather with Archie, a wire-haired vizsla. Both dogs had a lovely nature and were always fascinated with Millie and of course, vice versa. Sometimes we had chance meetings with Edward, another corgi. He'd pop out through a gap in the hedgerow. "Millie, now what do you make of that?" we asked. Edward was on holiday in Nottingham with his owner, and they stayed with one of her family in Watnall. Over the years we would bump into Edward and his owner, whose name I never found out! We would have long chats while the dogs would smell each other as if to say, "What sort of dog are you?"

Millie had lots of Labrador friends on our walks. An old boy, Benson, belonged to our neighbours, Sue and Ken. Benson was a lovely sandy colour, and he had a very gentle nature. Then there was Poppy, a black lab who we would sometimes meet on the fields with her owner, Jill. We enjoyed having a good chat about how the dogs were getting on. What was more important in life? Poppy always seemed to play a little rough with Millie, but nothing nasty. She always liked a little friendly sparring anyway! Millie always enjoyed the company of good-mannered dogs. By the way, is it just us? But we could meet the same people over and over with their dogs and yet, we only ever remembered the dog's name. Hardly ever the owner's name. How impolite!

Millie was such a huge part of our big family.

Millie was learning more and more about her surroundings, family, and friends. When we were out walking she began to choose her preferred route through the fields, through parts of the hedgerows which cut through to the next footpath. Left or right she chose, and why not? She knew where she was going! Once, when we were walking along a farm track near the woods in Watnall, Millie stopped at a gateway to nosey at what was beyond, and we carried on walking, knowing that she'd catch up with us. She eventually came running flat out past us and came to an abrupt stop a few yards in front of us. When we caught her up near a line of big puddles, she seemed a little mesmerised! "What are you looking at?" we asked, but it quickly became obvious. She'd noticed a reflection of herself in the water—did she think it was another dog? Either way, it was fascinating to watch her cocking her head from side to side like she did when you were explaining something. As I always carried a camera, I quickly captured another special moment. Walking on and with Millie back at our side, I asked, "Who was it you saw in there then, Mil?" We like to think that she knew it was an image of herself out for a walk with Mum and Dad!

In the woods we allowed her plenty of freedom to run quite a way in front. Then, not quite out of sight, she would suddenly look back at us: *Are you coming or not?* "Go on!" we'd shout, and she would immediately spring around and run again. What a lovely sight with her bobtail swinging to and fro like a pendulum. Running through the woods, she looked like she didn't have a care in the world!

Frisbees and Fish

One weekend in summertime we had decided to take Millie to the seaside with us. On the journey there, we briefly stopped at Sandringham to show Millie the house where her distant cousins stayed on holidays sometimes!

Millie waiting patiently to see her cousins!

We eventually arrived on the cliff top car park at Old Hunstanton on the east coast with Millie barking as she always seemed to know when we'd reached our destination.

It didn't take long to walk down from the car park to the beach. It was love at first sight for Millie; she stuck her nose in the air to take in the wonderful smell of the sea and off she went. Scampering, jumping through the puddles, careening towards the waves. She chased three or four seagulls that were never going to get caught!

Old Hunstanton has a wonderful beach and in the summer, the sea puddles are warm when the tide is out. We started walking towards where the waves were breaking and after almost having her nose nipped by a couple of small crabs hiding in the sand, Millie came dashing between us as fast as she could and splashed into the sea!

We started throwing the Frisbee into the water for her to retrieve and bring it back for us. She loved it, the waves and deep water didn't frighten her at all.

"Watch this!" I said to Elaine. I could see the waves coming in and timed the throw in the hope that Millie would catch the wave as well as the Frisbee! "Bring it!" I shouted to Millie. She jumped in after it and turned around just as the wave swept over her. Up she bobbed, head up and ears like sails, surfing like a pro. She hit the beach running, barrelling out of the water straight back around us and sat by our side with it in her mouth. And so, this was the afternoon game. She would bark and bark until we threw the Frisbee in again, time after time. That little dog loved it! Later that afternoon we returned to the car and gave Millie a good dry down with her towel, and she was able to shake the sand off very quickly.

Next stop, a traditional fish and chip shop.

"Yes, of course you can have some fish!" we said.

It was a very memorable day at the seaside, and fish

became one of her favourite tastes! To lick out a salmon or tuna tin was in her "Top Ten Tasty Things!" She only had to hear the sound of the tin opener punching the hole into the fish tin, and she would materialise by our side! I think that she always got a whiff of the fish before we did! Other favourites included cheese and liver cake, which Elaine made specially for her training tit-bits, and not forgetting her insistence on getting her snout into an empty yoghurt pot. We would hold onto it and turn it around and around until it was as clean as a whistle. Just the thing to save cleaning it before dropping it straight into the recycling bin! That nose of hers!

Tunnels, Tricks, and Tit-bits

Well, there we were, now practising for her silver award which was exciting, slowly going up the training ladder. Millie had already had a try at this test and didn't pass. I think it was on her "sit-stay" position. Anyway, the second time she tried, there were no problems, and she passed it in February, 2008. Cuddles and barking were the order of *that* day.

As time went on we heard from Polly that she was holding outdoor agility classes for all dogs on Sunday mornings. We asked if she thought Millie was up to it, and she said that she would certainly benefit from it. I'd always been fascinated watching dogs going around those set courses at the Crufts dog show on the television years ago, even before we ever thought about having a dog of our own. To be shown how to train your dog to perform and enjoy all the equipment that was available seemed to be a dream come true! We just couldn't wait!

Sunday morning came, and we arrived at the field where the agility course was all set up with jumps, tunnels, seesaws, an A-frame and a high bar. It looked like the owners were going to have to be quite agile too!

We were told to go around the course of jumps first. Millie jumped over the bars relatively easy—especially when she was following my left hand with treats in it! It was, "One, two, three, and follow me." To start with, I always found that Millie understood better if I stood at the third obstacle away from her, then called her to jump and lead her around to the last one. At the end of that, I'd always say, "Good girl, Millie!" and give her a fuss and a treat.

Then we tackled the tunnels. She just loved them, but we had a little hiccup to begin with…

We started from scratch, telling her to sit and wait at the entrance to give me time to get to the other end of the tunnel. With tit-bit in hand, I bent down and peered through; I could see her still waiting patiently.

"Millie, come, Millie, come!" I said.

But oh, dear! She ran around the tunnel instead! Next time she did the same again. *Okay, time to change tactics!* So we practised bringing Millie through my legs with a tit-bit in my hand. She followed the treat as she was drawn through the arch of my legs and at the same time, I commanded her by saying, "Through! Through!" Of course I couldn't forget to give her a treat immediately and tell her what a good girl she was!

Now for the tricky bit! I told her to sit a little way from the tunnel entrance again so that I could stand with legs astride at the entrance.

"Millie, through! Millie, through!"

It did the trick! As she went under my legs I carried on shouting, "Through! Through! Through!" until she popped out at the other end of the tunnel all excited with her barking head on! That was worth three treats. She soon got the hang of it after that. It wasn't long before I stood facing the entrance with Millie sitting at my side. I'd point towards the entrance and say, "Through, Millie!" Away she went as fast as she could through the tunnel like a rabbit! It wasn't long before she no longer needed tit-bits to run through it.

Onto the high beam. She was so trusting. We would always walk beside her ready for any accident, like a fall. She took each little step with care and with so much confidence and ability. After a couple of sessions she was going up and across the beam like an experienced tightrope walker! We were told that in competitions, dogs were supposed to stop at the bottom line that was marked out on the beam so we had a go at that. After numerous attempts, she learned to stop at the line before jumping to the ground. And yes, you caught us, she did have one or two tit-bits for her trouble…or was it three?

And then, to the seesaw; a slow walk up the middle then we instructed Millie to wait as the bar pivoted down. At that point, we'd say, "Millie, come." and encourage her to walk down to the end. We'd then call, "Wait!" before telling her to "Jump!" After two or three times she clicked on what we wanted her to do and seemed to love it. With a fast wagging bobtail, you could tell she was so excited!

"Do you think she would go up the A-frame?" Polly asked.

What? Where Alsatians go up and over? "I don't know."

"Try her!" Polly said.

Never in a million years did I think that I would be running at the side of a dog attempting to run up an A-frame on a canine agility course, let alone a little corgi!

But, with a little bit of a scramble at the top, up and over she went. She was so excited once she was there! And we had a wonderful time too. We progressed enough to be timed going around the complete course that was set up at the end of the session. In the end she went to several of these meetings, and I thoroughly enjoyed it, never mind Millie! Who would need to enter in triathlons when you can compete in these events with your dog! For a novice at this, Millie was well up in time with the front runners! Being here amongst other owners and their dogs was something special again, and it was a real learning platform for Millie. We took her there just to see how she would get on…and she did it all!

Injury Strikes—Pool Time!

One November morning, we were coming home from her usual walk up and over the hill at the back of Trough Lane, and we met one of her springer spaniel friends, Megan. Her owner, Sue, chatted to us and the dogs played about together as they usually did. Millie was just being her usual lairy self running around Megan. She slightly skidded out, rolled over on the slope, and yelped.

"What have you done now?" I shouted.

We picked her up and had a good look to see if she had anything stuck in her paw, such as a thorn or a cut from a fragment of glass, but nothing was visible. She managed to walk home okay, although she was limping on her back leg.

We took her to the vets in Eastwood. After examination they thought that Millie had sprained her cruciate ligament in her left back leg. *Oh, dear!* The vet recommended a specialist team in Castle Donnington.

After making an appointment we took her the following day. It was as our vet had said, cruciate ligament damage and she would need an operation. No long walks and try to keep her calm were our orders, and we were to put some anti-inflammatory tablets in her food. The following week we took her for the operation and left her overnight.

When we picked her up again the surgeon said everything went all right, and he was sure that the joint would heal quickly and be strong again soon. We could not thank him enough and lifted Millie up to carry her out to the car.

"No, no! Let her walk slowly on lead. She needs to use her leg now. Just take it steady."

Two or three weeks went by, and Millie didn't seem to progress in her walking. We could see that she was unhappy about this. So, we took her back to our vet. She said that the muscle had wasted down a little because she wasn't using it enough. She recommended that we take her to the Nottingham Canine Hydrotherapy Clinic in Hucknall.

The folks there were brilliant and very professional. This was where our days with Millie at the coast came in handy as she showed no fear of the water. The staff put her on a harness and lowered her into the pool. Most animals do the doggie paddle instinctively before they even enter the water, but Millie looked as though we'd just wound her up like a clockwork model boat. The propellers on those little boats always whizzed around before you put them into the water. Millie's legs were going like bee wings, and she hit the water running!

As soon as Steve, one of the hydrotherapists, put her in the water she was away like a torpedo. We were still worried about her muscle loss on her leg and wondered how long it would be before she could build it up. But we had no need to worry or be sceptical about the treatment. In just four weeks we could see that her leg was getting to the same build as her other leg, and she was walking a lot better. The hydrotherapists were very happy with her. Even when she was fit, we took her every month for a little swim because she loved it so much.

We eased off on her training a little, and she enjoyed her walks again, but we had to be careful about things such as jumping. When anyone came to the door, she would launch herself off the arm of the chair (one of her favourite perches) and tear towards them. She couldn't understand why we were telling her off when she was doing something we'd always let her do before, but it wasn't too long before she was back to normal.

Millie was always a bit of a daredevil. Only silly things, such as the Dyson cleaner, put her off her stride. For some reason this was the monster in the house. Even after all her training and spending time with her and the Dyson, even putting treats on it for her to retrieve, she refused to put up with it! Whenever we used it, we would send her out of the room. To her, that coupled with the plug-click sound meant monster on the loose. Why? We will never know; all dogs have their little foibles. But this was very much when she got her barking head on!

The cruciate ligament injury delayed her training for her gold award. After a few months off we went to training again, and it wasn't long before test day. Millie always showed an interest in whatever she was asked to do. It was really exciting on test days when dogs were doing their stuff. On one occasion a lovely dog called Archie, who behaved as mischievous as he looked, happened to be doing very well in a certain part of a test he was in (which was all to do with his food manners). Archie was to walk to his owner and ignore the two food dishes full of biscuits between them. Archie did this brilliantly, but one time was very memorable. He walked beyond the bowls of biscuits like a good boy, went to his owner, and sat down in front of him as he'd been trained. His owner gave Archie his titbits for being a good boy but that wasn't enough for Archie! He immediately jumped up, flew back to the bowls, and scoffed the lot! Hilarious! What a character!

I'm happy to say that Millie passed her gold. Well done, her!

Cat Flaps and Pheasant Chases

We'd planned for Millie to stay with our son and daughter-in-law, Carl and Carlie, and our grandchildren, Chloe, Sam, and Emily for about a week while we went abroad on holiday.

When we were on our way to the airport we had a call.

"Hello, do you own a corgi?" the lady asked. "Because I've just found one wandering down our road, and I found your phone number on the disc on her collar."

Carl and Carlie knew that Millie wasn't in the house, and they'd assumed she was outside somewhere. They were looking for her when we got the call from the lady who'd stopped in her car. It was very kind of her. Elaine told the lady where Millie was staying, and we called Carl and Carlie to see what had happened. They guessed that Millie must have seen one of the cats going through the cat-flap in the kitchen door and probably thought, *I can do that*. So out she went and up the path. They made sure she couldn't try that again! We phoned the lady back later and thanked her once more for her help. Knowing she was safe again, we carried on to the airport and had a lovely break.

Another time when we were staying with them, I

was walking Millie in the garden. She was exploring and made a dash for the stream running through it.

"Come on now, Millie, it's bedtime. Stop playing about. It's all dark down there!" I shouted.

She must have heard movement in the undergrowth down the banking and wanted to discover what it was. It could have been a hedgehog or a toad, anything like that, but it wasn't the time to be playing cat and mouse with anything. *Right! Time to use the correct language!*

"Millie, come! Millie, come!" I turned and walked back to the house and raised my voice a little. "Millie, heel! Millie, heel!" I said and patted my left leg. There she was, at my side straight away! All that work put in at training certainly showed at the times when it wasn't really too important, but it always helped! Millie knew what the important words were and how it was said! "Good girl," I said again, but when we took her in the conservatory, we knew that she had been paddling in the mud at the side of the stream. "Millie! What are you like? Look at the state of you!"

I think she noticed that we were trying not to laugh while we set about cleaning her up!

***

Another time when we went down to stay with Carl, Carlie, and the grandchildren, we were all taking Millie for a walk in the woods. We'd been strolling along for about five minutes when she stopped suddenly in front of us. About three yards away from her on an old tree trunk stood a beautiful cock pheasant. It was positioned perfectly in a sunbeam that looked like a spotlight coming through the leafy canopy of the trees. It shone directly on to the bird and made it look like a jewelled brooch! It seemed to freeze for a second like we all did…but not for long!

I suppose Millie thought, *I want it!* She jumped forward like a flash and went into a run. The pheasant was half flying and running at the same time, as they do. (I'm not sure pheasants always understand that they can actually fly!). They both disappeared around a bend in the pathway. We soon caught up and saw that the bird had flown over a deep cutting and landed on another tree behind us. The pheasant was getting the full force of Millie's barking and her "moonwalk-strutting-her-stuff" style. Chase over. I quickly took a picture of Millie looking over at the pheasant with that *want it* look! From that day on, any mention of pheasant put Millie into overdrive with a quick run and looking around as if to say, "Where is it?"

Millie loved posing for photos in settings as beautiful as she was.

Our Girl Goes Platinum

Over time she had several attempts at her platinum award. Two of the stages in this test were to teach your dog to take the lid off a saucepan, retrieve the contents to take to their owner, go back to the saucepan and replace the lid. This exercise was quite a feat to expect your dog to carry out with only two or three tries. Repeatedly we put her small plastic dumbbell toy into the saucepan without the lid on and told her to bring it back. We played with this dumbbell a lot, and when she brought it back, we would give her the usual "Good girl" fuss straight away. She would always want to bring it back in case there was a chance of a gravy bone! Sometimes we'd hide it and ask her to find it and bring it back. This was also be rewarded with a tasty treat now and again, and it kept her on her toes! We took this exercise even further by letting her see us place the lid over the dumbbell in the saucepan whilst she was next to it and then tell her to get it. Eventually she was determined to get to it. She grabbed hold of the handle, lifted the lid, and threw it out of the way! Her head disappeared into the saucepan and out she'd pop with the dumbbell! She had got it and never forgot it! She always put two and two together very quickly. Later we tied an old sock onto the handle so she could get hold of it easier.

Another part of the test was to train your dog to walk through your legs while you were walking with a slight stride and also to teach your dog to do a twirl on demand. This was a very repetitive part of the training. I may have mentioned before, but we kept up with the fun side of things and showed her that we were always having a good and happy time in these training sessions. She picked up on that. Walking in and out of our legs was attained by having a treat such as a little liver cake on the end of a small rod. Walking slowly, we would put the tit-bit near Millie's nose and draw it through my legs with her following, wanting the treat! Not until she had carried out a good movement, with me calling out, "Through, Millie. Through, Millie!" did a treat appear! Getting her to do her twirls was assisted with a treat on the end of a rod, letting her follow the circling motion to the left and then to the right, coupled with voice instructions. We also taught her to do her roly-polys and twirls clockwise and anti-clockwise! We always believed that perseverance and patience would bring rewards. This sort of training was all part of her journey through life. We enjoyed seeing how she thrived on learning anything! What laughs, enjoyment, and barking we had in training sessions!

Practice makes perfect, they say, and that certainly worked for Millie. It wasn't all her fault when something went wrong in her test.

"As you can all see, it's not just the dog making the mistakes. It's the owner that's rusty!" Polly would often say. Or did she say rubbish?

Millie loved going to her training at the Nuthall Church Hall and at Brinsley Parish Hall. Whenever her training gear (jumps, cones, and bags) were being loaded into the car, she would lie crocodile-style near the door with a “Come on! Hurry up” stare.

On reaching her training venue she would excitedly bark a little before we arrived. She knew that there were a lot of friends at these meetings and lots of treats. I’d say “Wait” at the doors to get in first and then say, “Good girl, Millie. Come!” Once we were in and settled, we always made that little bond by getting Millie to do the watch exercise (Elaine continually trained her to do this when we were at home carrying out her first training exercises), then we were ready to take on all the exercises.

So, there we were, starting the Platinum test yet again. Everything went all right apart from the “stand-stay” exercise again. We tried all sorts of things to help Millie to understand. I think she found this part of the exercise a little boring but nevertheless she had to learn to obey her command.

Six weeks later, in October 2008, we tried again after painstakingly practising the stand-stay position. What a relief it was when she completed that perfectly and had that sort of *“What’s all the fuss about? It’s simple to do that!”* look on her face (chewing on a small piece of liver cake, of course!).

Our Little Socialite

Our little canine friend was really maturing into such a clever dog. Her sense of smell and hearing were really spot on. When she combined the two, it was truly amazing. How on earth did she know when an Alsatian named Bear was being walked on the footpath outside our house by his mum and dad?

Bear, Millie's first crush.

Even without any barking from him she always knew he was there and made a fuss, with a few barks and many spin-arounds. She never made a fuss when other dogs walked by outside, only for Bear. He was a handsome dog with a gorgeous coat, and I think Millie might've had a little crush on him. We always told him that he was a good boy whenever we met on walks. I think both dogs were just curious about each other but kept their distance. Respect, I think, is the word!

We always tried to take Millie with us whenever we could, whether that was shopping, visiting friends, or holidays where possible. If we couldn't, we knew there was always a special welcome waiting for us when we came home. When we entered the house she would sometimes run off to collect one of her favourite toys which would be near her bed. It would be either her two-tone yellow elephant or a brown puppy dog with big floppy ears. We never knew which one she would run back to us with, but for a bit of fun we always tried to guess and we would be shouting out whatever she was going to bring to us. What a performance and what a welcome. She had the elephant from being a pup, and once upon a time it was nearly twice as big as she was. The puppy she won, at one of Polly's fun days in a competition.

Sometimes when we went on holiday without her she stayed with our neighbours, Sue and Jason. When the cases were packed and standing in the hall, she would skulk into her crocodile position, and we're sure she was wondering where we were off to. There was never a problem leaving her especially if she was just staying next door. Sue told us that Millie would always remember where the biscuits were in the kitchen. We later learnt that they were the McVitie's digestives that she would receive with that sort of "Please can I have?"

look! Spoilt or what?! Even if it was only a small piece to munch on!

Once, we were ready to go and saying our good-byes, Millie leapt through the front doorway of Sue and Jason's. It was as if she was saying, "Hurry up with your good-byes, there's biscuits to be had here!" Greedy girl! Millie knew she could bend the rules in this household a little! Sue always said that she was fun to look after and such a good girl. When walking her, Sue said that although Millie walked well with them on her lead and quickly returned to them when she had been let off with only a call of, "Millie, come!" she would sometimes tug on the lead as if she was telling them, "Go this way...not that way!"

"Oi! Behave!" Sue said, telling her straight, but with a hidden smile. We always looked forward to coming home from holiday to share Millie's excitement.

Millie had a very busy social life. Now and again she would stay with our other son and daughter-in-law, James and Nic, at Gamston, the other side of Nottingham. Our granddaughters, Ella and Lexi, were always eager to play with her and accompany their mum and dad when taking her for a walk by their local canal. Millie had fun with the ducks but always gave the swans a wide berth, clever enough not to make eye contact with them. It must have been instinct. She was always as good as gold, apart from one night when Millie thought it would be a good game if Nic had to chase her around the lawn to bring her in after her last wee at night in the dark. She finally succumbed to the lure of a special biscuit. Naughty girl!

***

Summertime again meant another trip to the seaside,

this time for a week. We stayed at a lovely cottage on the sea road at Brancaster near Hunstanton. We always had a lovely time whenever we went to the East Coast. Over time, Millie learnt all the footpaths around there, and oh, how we all loved the early morning walks on the coastal path. I've often wondered how dogs remember all that. Even after a year's break Millie would know exactly what was around the corner on the cliff tops. We would get out of the car, and Millie would tear down the path onto that lovely beach and run as fast as she could into the waves. She loved it! And so did we! This time we stopped off at Sandringham, where of course, she received a lot of Royal welcomes from people, especially children.

Once when we stopped there was a bus party of American tourists who were walking by us as we sat outside having a cup of tea at one of the tables of the cafe.

"Gee, is that one of the Queen's dogs?" one of them shouted to us.

"It might be," I said back jokingly, and instantly they all crowded around wanting pictures taken with her. Millie loved the attention and danced in and out of their children's legs. They loved it, and I think Millie helped to make their day. One of the ladies came and gave a special thank you to Millie and us.

"We sure have a doggie tale to tell the folks back home!"

"You're welcome!" I said, committing it to mind as another memorable moment. We walked around to the main gate of the road to Sandringham House and took some photos of her in front of those well-known gates. Ever the poser, Millie would have made the Queen proud if she had been one of her dogs!

Though she loved her holidays, she loved coming

home just as much, and she seemed to scoot all around the house and outside as if making sure everything was still in its rightful place. *I've had a lovely time, but it's great to be back.*

***

Millie was growing ever more into a mature dog and loved being amongst children, especially another one of our grandsons, Harrison. We would look after him sometimes in the week and Millie would follow him around like a shadow. Even though Millie was a lovely calm dog, we always had the rule that no dog should be left alone with a baby or child. When another one of our four sons, Ian and partner Tara came to pick Harrison up she would bark and lick and run around as if saying, "I've been looking after him as well."

Time marched on. Walking through autumn leaves in the woods Millie was sometimes quite camouflaged in those lovely golden, red, and yellow leaves she sank into up to her tummy. Once or twice, Millie would be somewhere and do something, and it would bring back a tender memory of our little dog, Honey! Two dogs are never the same, but we knew that they would have been the best of friends. Sometimes Millie would catch one or two leaves when a breeze would persuade them to drizzle down from the canopy high above.

Winter walks were always an adventure when it had been snowing. As with most dogs, snow had such a fascination for Millie; lots of different shapes and gaps in hedgerows filled in and smoothed over by the wind. She used to plough through the snow in winter with her nose and jump for snowballs thrown into the air for her. When she'd jumped up and obliterated them, she always seemed bewildered as to where they'd vanished to!

I recall one occasion where we trekked up to the top of the hill on the back field and came upon an igloo! Built by children and parents by the looks of it! It must have been the highest igloo in Nottinghamshire! Millie ran around and came to an abrupt stop near the entrance.

Standing guard at her igloo castle.

"What's in there, Mil?" I shouted.

She hunched up on her hind quarters, squatted down on her chest, and barked into the tunnel of the entrance of this thing that shouldn't be there, on *her* hilltop! Danger was here, or so she thought, because we couldn't coax her to having a nosey inside even by throwing in a treat.

Leaps, Bounds, and Dancing

Christmas was soon here and gone again and a New Year began. Training Millie was always interesting. We could see her improving on sections of her test each time she tried. It was really satisfying to see how much she enjoyed it, and she seemed to thrive on it.

Springtime saw another attempt at the Platinum two test. Millie appeared to be ready for this one. But were we? Well, one of the exercises was dancing to music. After thinking about one or two old pop tunes we plumped for "Poetry in Motion" which was recorded by Johnny Tillotson and was one of my favourites in the 1960's—it fitted the bill perfectly. If you ever get the chance to listen to this song, you'll see how we managed to get a little dance routine going quite easily to the rhythm of this catchy sixties' music.

Millie really let loose. As soon as Elaine put the music on, I sent Millie to the end of the hall and signalled for her to stay. When the singing began, I pointed at Millie and jumped up and spun around with my back to her. After practising for a couple of months, she knew that was her signal to run to me and run straight through my legs. She'd dance to the music with her twirls and roly-polys, in and out of my steps and walk with me, jumping over my outstretched leg;

all things we had practised at home and in the training sessions. It was another event in our lives where Millie had just started to allow us a little sprinkle of limelight. She was, as that song went, "walking by my side" and she was "poetry in motion" as we made the dance up to the music, using her knowledge of movements to commands I gave quickly and quietly. The object was to make all the movements flow together. At the end of this session I think we must have given a not too bad show, as we received quite good round of applause from other dog handlers watching. It proved to be the first of many entertaining performances in front of an audience for our little friend!

Finding fake drugs in the form of tea bags and Brillo pads was another part of this test. The items were placed in various places in the hall, and Millie had to find them, lie down, and keep on barking, which she did! She was wonderful at this exercise, so quick and determined. But, *oh dear,* after all this brilliant work she let herself down on the simplest of exercises, the stand-stay. Well, the Platinum two award had to wait for the future. A fail on any one part of this test makes it a total fail! We decided that Millie would show us when she was ready to crack all parts of this test at the same time. After all, as the saying goes, practise makes perfect.

When we had visitors we would sometimes let her perform one of her party tricks. She was always eager to show off especially if a treat was being offered.

One of Millie's breakfast treats was apple segments from our own breakfast topping. She would wait by the side of whoever was making breakfast for her share of the apple pieces, with no barking or begging aloud! That early training when she was a puppy certainly helped her with her meal time manners. Once her portion of eight small pieces was singled out, we would tell her to wait while we went into the lounge to hide them. With a call of, “Find ‘em, Mil,” she would scamper through the hall into the lounge and set her sensitive nose to work. All gone in five minutes or less, no problem! This was a daily ritual. Sometimes she would spin around while she was waiting, if the apples were really tasty, like those Jazz apples. She loved this little morning ritual. Collecting instant rewards for using her sense of smell wasn’t a bad way to start her day!

Wiping her down from a walk in the rain was usually a simple task. I’d start with a request of, “Shake!” And she would just do that, wetting you through in the process! A command to “Lie down and let me look at you” was followed with “Good girl.” Eventually Millie learned to lay on her back to have her tummy wiped dry, while I’d be saying, “Look at you, Mil, look at you!” Obviously a clean up after a walk was a lot easier when the weather was dry.

But whatever the weather, Millie got us out and about in the elements. If she came back home after being in the fields and the woods on a wet day and she was filthy, she went straight into the baby bath we had in the garage. Her legs would be going ten to the dozen as we lowered her into the warm water that just had a small amount of doggie shampoo added. I think she was practising her swimming. Once she’d been dried off as much as possible she would dive into the kitchen and run around the house. She was so fussy, drying and licking herself, as if we hadn’t done it properly!

A little tip here on the training side. We found that connecting a sound with a natural action that your dog is already doing is a good start in getting a good response from a command. An example of this would be when Millie first gave herself a good shake after a bit of a soaking, we immediately shouted, “Shake! Shake!

Shake!" Even if you think that this might be a slightly back to front way of training, it certainly worked for Millie! She soon learned to carry out the action related to that word! We once caught Millie coming backwards out of the gap between the lounge wall and the settee. At the same time, we both started saying, "Walk back! Walk back!" Millie soon put two and two together. We found that small helpings of tying commands together with what she was already doing on her own really bolstered her intelligence involving sounds with actions. Millie became an expert on the positioning in the sit-stand-stay on the move exercise, which was basically commanding a dog to position itself in a certain manner while the owner carried on walking or even running away when taking the platinum test. She really loved this one in her training! Even when you carried on walking away from her just to shout, "Heel!" would release her from her last command, and wherever we were in the hall, she'd come trotting to our side and under control. This exercise had to be perfect for test day! Sometimes in training, a favourite tit-bit was allowed! We always made sure hand, arm, and voice were always in unison when we instructed Millie. We tried to give our little canine friend as much time as we could and involve her in our life. We just couldn't help it! Like I've said before, most pets but especially a dog, will give you so much back for a little love and always be there for you.

The next year was busy as usual, including more trips to the East Coast including a delightful place called Happisburgh (pronounced Aysborough). We would say to Millie that she was going to "Happy-burg" for lots of walking along the cliff tops and around the lighthouse. The walk along the path to the lighthouse was one of those special places that we were making a lovely memory. As soon as we turned onto this path everything just clicked into place for the perfect scene for us. Our little girl, so happy, running along this winding path leading right up to the lighthouse buildings. At the time the tall grass was blowing about in long waves to the tune of the sea breeze blowing across the top of the cliffs. Millie just loved it, especially when the fur around the back of her little pendulum tail was wafted about every now and then. Millie was always excited when she was in unknown territory. She was a natural explorer, but always checked that we weren't far away. Yet another beautiful walk on a lovely sunny day meant another fine memory captured. Later, we just had to take her for a run on the beach and a swim. It was a lovely place. It's such a pity that the cliffs are now eroding there at an astonishing rate.

Millie loved getting her paws wet and sandy.

***

Christmas parties at dog training were a favourite, with plenty of obedience games for dogs and owners. What fun there was to be had. One of the sections of the party was to fancy dress your dog. We'd never really been keen on the dressing up of animals as it adds nothing to a clever canine. Nevertheless, as it was a Christmas party, we played along. We came up with the idea of dressing Millie up in her national costume, an idea taken from a small pottery figure of a corgi reared up on its hind legs and dressed in a Welsh costume that we'd acquired from an antiques shop while we were on holiday. We made Millie a black hat trimmed with white lace and a cape to match. Although she came second in that competition, she looked every bit a little Welsh girl. What a picture, and it was a lovely memorable evening for us handlers. Thank you, Polly!

And so into the New Year of 2012 we went, with one or two ideas starting to come to mind. We could just tell that Millie loved to be amongst people. Okay, we admit it. We loved to show her off because she was so well behaved and full of fun. Why not share her talents with others and put little shows together and probably earn a little something for charities as well?

Top of the Class

We put more work into her training this year as we wanted Millie to achieve what she deserved. That extra special Platinum two award was just there for her to be had. *Come on, Millie. We know you can do it*. There was no room for slip ups on this one. Send-a way, recalls, finding drugs, sit, stay down, around the cones one way and then the other. And we knew about the twirls and the roly-polys and the dancing to music, but what about that stand and stay?!

Everything had to be performed to the letter. Most of the categories in the test were much the same, but dog and handler needed to concentrate as the stays were longer, and several alterations were made to make it more difficult.

We did lots of training at home, and we would sometimes bring Millie to heel and practice some of her training exercises on our walks in the countryside and on the parks, which she seemed to love.

The day came for Millie to have another try at passing this last rung on the aptitude awards' ladder. Throughout the exercises and with the way she was reacting to commands that evening, I knew she could do something special.

Well, there we were out of the car and Millie with

her barking head on! Brinsley Parish Hall was the venue and it was test night. The kingpin was the stand-stay out of sight exercise, and this always seemed to be a little problem for Millie. We thought that she had a niggly ache since her operation for cruciate ligament damage. She seemed to find it more comfortable to sit than to stand in the same position for a time, or was I just finding excuses? I don't know. Also, perhaps she found that exercise boring. I know I did! Anyway, we had extra practice on this with an extra special treat. Eventually Polly, the trainer, opened the door of the hall where we were all waiting to be called back into the main room. Everyone went out of the porch and up to their dogs which left me on my own. *Come on, Millie. We know you can do it!*

The Platinum two award takes longer than other tests, so I was the only one left in the hallway taking part in it and wondering how Millie was getting on with me out of sight. Oh the waiting! Quite possibly the longest two minutes of my life!

The hall door opened.

"Millie is still standing! She's completed all the test!" Polly shouted.

"Hallelujah!" I said striding back into the hall. I gave her a big cuddle. "Who's a clever girl, then?" Of course, I gave her the special treat that I'd promised her: a piece of Jazz apple and a little chunk of liver cake. And she was looking for it, the little monkey! All the way home I told her how clever she was, though never forgetting to tell her when we were approaching the tight bends around Moorgreen reservoir. Millie never roamed around the back of the car. She always stayed put on the rear seat behind the driver as she'd been taught. But still, I always warned her about sharp bends by saying, "Going around" loudly. She would brace herself. She *loved* going for a ride with Mum and Dad.

"Well, that was exhausting."

We were as proud as punch for her that night. *Well done, Millie*. She certainly deserved it after all that hard work practising. We decided to take a nice walk the next day through the local woods and up and over the hills, to reflect on everything our furry friend had attained. Little did we know what the future held for her.

It's Showtime

A couple of months later we were talking to a friend called Marian, who we first met at the APT School for Dogs and who had a brilliant Jack Russell called Dill. What a character he was. Very sharp witted and smart, and of course, never naughty...well, not really! Marian told us that her mother was in a care home for the elderly in Eastwood, and that sometimes people brought dogs into the home for a little fuss. She said that it was a calming and comforting experience for the residents. I immediately wondered if it was something Millie could do, but the residents would get the bonus of being amused and entertained with her agility tricks.

A few days later, we called in on the home to see if they might be interested in Millie visiting. They'd already been told about Millie by Marian, and they were more than happy to say, "Absolutely!"

So, the date was set. Because Millie was a corgi, we had the idea to give her show a royal theme, particularly as it was the Queen's Jubilee year. We pulled together several props such as a crown-shaped piece of linen for her to find amongst several standard sized pieces. We adapted part of her training (to retrieve an object out of a saucepan and then go back and put the lid back on) into

Millie helping with the dinner at Buckingham Palace!

We gave her a lot of extra training for this so that she would bring back first a carrot, then go back to the saucepan for a broccoli head, and lastly for a potato, all out of the same pot on demand. We were amazed at how quickly Millie learned the word associated with each different vegetable, how it smelled, and what it looked like. It was very repetitive training over many hours, but Millie took it in her stride, and it was another one of those fun things she just loved to do! I remember though, at one show, she was supposed to pull out a carrot and pulled out a potato instead. We looked at each other, and Millie simply opened her mouth and dropped the potato back in the pot. She then went back into the pot for the right vegetable and was rewarded with riotous applause. Sometimes the mistakes were more fun than when she got it right! We added a little music to go with the performance, and it was a right royal success. Millie was so excited by all the fuss, and everyone in the room clapped and laughed at her antics. All of this was surrounded with bunting, patriotic flags, and one or two pictures of corgis and the Queen, of course. It was just so satisfying to see our little Millie giving so much pleasure to a lot of people. From then on, we knew that there had to be more to come.

While all this was happening, our son, Peter, and his partner, Alicia, were staying with us for a while on a long holiday (from Australia). Millie really hit it off with these two. She would immediately jump up between them on the sofa when she could. It was as if she knew they wouldn't be around for long. She would look at Elaine or myself as if to say, "They like me sat here, so there!" To be fair, she was just the same with our son, Ian, and his partner, Tara. She'd welcome them with a bark and a cheek-lick when she sat between them! We would only tell her off for jumping up onto the sofa when she'd come into the house straight off the lawn, with a shout of, "Oi, get down, Millie!" Once Peter and Alicia went off on their travels to Europe, any mention of their name and Millie would look around as if they might appear at any moment.

A couple of months after coming back from Europe, they told us that they were going back to Australia to live. It was a time of sad good-byes all around, and it was four long years before we were able to visit them.

Months later, we were walking up one of the hills close by.

"Can you remember Millie chasing Peter to the top of this hill?" I asked Elaine. Suddenly Millie was off like a shot to the top of the hill. Staying in sight of us she was looking all around her as if to say, "Where? Where's Peter?" Bless her.

Peter and Alicia had to also say good-bye to the two new additions to our family, Isobel, the daughter of Ian and Tara, and Lexi, James' and Nic's new daughter. But these two turned out to be more helpers for Millie's tricks. As Isobel grew older she learned to make Millie wait for her food till she was told, "Good girl," while pointing down to her bowl.

Word started to travel about Millie and her little shows, and we were contacted by Sheila Longdon at The Spinney, a care home in Nuthall. She asked if we could do our show there, and we were delighted to say yes.

Millie was always eager to enter the buildings where she seemed to know that she was going to entertain and have some fun! She would like a little Hoover around first, under the tables and chairs for hidden crumbs, and then she'd focus on the people. Then she'd introduce herself in her own special way with a bark and a lick. "I'm here!" Everyone fell in love with

Millie at first sight. "Isn't she a pretty little dog?" was a constant refrain. She never lost her puppy looks. *Lucky girl!*

Once all the excitement of meeting new people was done with, she was a wonder. It was basically a lot of her original training, with some bits added here and there to make her show more fun. She was such a joy to watch. As time went on, she picked up all the extra tricks within weeks.

When I had Millie's attention, I would nod to Elaine and we would begin. She would put the music on for that particular part of her show, such as Bobby Vee singing "Rubber ball" when she was running through the long tunnel over the jumps and collecting three balls out of a bowl. We were trying to raise money for charity, so we ran a lottery. This entailed putting the first three numbers that were picked out of the box onto the balls that Millie would retrieve. The first ball that Millie returned was the winner, then second, and so on. It was a little twist on a lottery, but it made it a lot more fun for everyone!

We thought that it might be a good idea to tell the local press about what Millie was doing locally. Sheila, from the Spinney, said that sometimes a local journalist, Peter Jordan, attended their functions and wrote small articles for the local newspapers. She told us to give him a ring to see if he could attend some of Millie's performances.

So we did. We called Peter, and he gave us such a lot of help. He even captioned some of the photographs. We can't praise him enough. He turned up for us all over the place at all sorts of times! Thank you again, Peter! Most of Millie's shows at the Care Homes ended with Millie being fussed by the residents and staff. Elaine always accompanied this with a little "Magic Moments" by Perry Como or "Give me Sunshine" by Morecambe and Wise, which most of the residents knew. Elaine always knew exactly the right music to play for every occasion!

Millie Goes National

So now the local press (The Kimberley and Eastwood Advertiser, The Hucknall Despatch and Nottingham Evening Post) were always interested in the stories of Millie's exploits, even naming her "Millie Corgi the Wonder Dog." It wasn't too long before one or two national magazines wanted the story of our clever corgi. In the end we told our doggy tale to Yours magazine. They'd been looking for a corgi that was just that bit special, and they were putting out an eight-page supplement in their special Jubilee edition. Seeing that Millie's shows had a royal theme, it was just the ticket for them.

They sent a photographer from Peterborough to take some shots of her, and before we knew it, Millie was on the front cover with her picture next to the Queen's, and two pages covering Millie's story or should we say, exploits.

Afterwards the magazine was kind enough to send a cheque to our charity at the time, Sense, the Deaf/Blind Association. We arranged a meeting with the charity's shop manager at the Hucknall branch so we could pass on all the donations that we had collected up to that time: the princely sum of £399.75. We took Millie with us to the shop for a photo shoot with the cheque that we prepared specially. Peter Jordon, a local photographer, was there to capture the moment. Sense were delighted with the money Millie's efforts had raised!

Millie "paws" over the cheque to local charity, Sense.

We began to get phone calls from all over the country. Amongst those was one from my sister, Ann, in Worthing. She'd just picked up a copy of the magazine and had been showing everyone in the shop that her brother and sister-in-law owned the little corgi featured in the supplement. Ann and her husband, Ron, always made a fuss of Millie when they came up to Nottingham to visit us and vice versa. Whenever they came to stay, Millie always found their bedroom in the morning to tell them when it was breakfast time! Ron said that sometimes in the night he would hear the door of the bedroom give a whispering creak, and he knew that it was Millie checking out on her overnight family visitors. She didn't bother them at all, but we think that she was just making sure that they were okay and safe in *her* house! She never slept in their bedroom but would position herself to one side of the doorway on the landing as if on guard!

Out of the blue we had a call from Mrs Jameson of Wharryton's where we had Millie from. Apparently one of her friends had phoned her to say that she'd just seen one of her dogs in a magazine and that Wharryton's had been mentioned. She remembered Millie and got in touch. She was so glad that one of her pups had got on so well. We always knew that Millie had a lovely start in her life being born into such a wonderful atmosphere surrounded by her family. These early days are so important.

On the 30th July, 2011, Millie swam non-stop for ten minutes at the Nottingham Canine Hydrotherapy Centre to help to raise money for Brain Tumour Research at Nottingham's Q.M.C. and the Lincolnshire and Nottinghamshire Air Ambulance. The following year she was asked to swim again, and she loved every minute of it!

One day in a training class in 2012, we were talking to a friend, Gloria Morgan, who had just had published a book about her rescue dog, Cassie. She gave a lot of love and care, including training, to Cassie. I can remember when Gloria first brought her along to training classes. Cassie would take refuge under Gloria's chair, slightly withdrawn and keeping her distance from the other dogs. After only a couple of months Cassie was learning that there were lots of friends out there to say hello to, and she lost her fear and shyness. All Gloria's love and hard work certainly gave Cassie a new life.

Anyway, Gloria was president of the Farmers Market in Kimberley at that time and they were having a special party at the Kimberley Parish Hall with a dancing group and a choir performing. Gloria knew that Millie had been performing shows, and she asked if we would let Millie perform that evening. I think Millie gave the folks there a lot of enjoyment that night. We had such a lot of laughs as we'd started to incorporate all kinds of spin-off tricks. For instance, one little trick was to tell her audience that I was forever losing my keys. Elaine would take Millie outside the door, and I'd tell the audience that Millie had to be taken out of the room because she would cheat if she could! I hid my keys somewhere in the hall on the floor out of easy sight. Elaine brought Millie in again, and I talked about the show. At the same time I patted my trouser pockets without saying that I'd lost my keys. I looked around and said, "Oh, no!" Immediately Millie picked up on this and began her search for Dad's keys. When she had found them she brought them straight back, shaking her head to and fro to jangle the keys and waggling her little pendulum tail. She was so chuffed with herself—and rightly so! That little trick garnered lots of clapping from the audience.

We also brought into this show her drug finding ability, with a tea bag and a Brillo pad standing in for an illegal substance! With Millie out of the room, we hid the items in the room on top of a chair or tucked into someone's shoe. Elaine then brought her back into the room, and she sat in front of me.

"Millie! Drugs!" I said. She immediately went off on a search and very soon she let me know where the drugs were by lying down and barking like mad, pointing at them with her nose. She didn't attempt to touch the offending, substance as she'd been trained not to do in her Platinum test. What another lovely evening that was; a proper variety show with music and dancing.

We had a funny thing happen at another one of her

shows. It was a very mixed-age audience, and we were doing the drug search routine. Elaine brought Millie into the hall as usual. I gave the command to search, and she made a bee-line for a young lady's handbag. A mistake surely, because who takes a Brillo pad or tea bags to a show? Millie sniffed at it for about a minute without barking.

A little order of "Millie. Find drugs," again, and Millie continued on with her search. After successfully locating both items with a good barking session she received her applause.

After the show, the young lady with the handbag walked up to Elaine.

"Why did your dog start to look and sniff around my handbag for a long time?" she asked with a worried expression.

We explained the whole point of the exercise again and suggested that her handbag probably smelled of tea or Brillo pads. We had to wonder though, had Millie inadvertently become a real drug sniffer dog and the young lady had another substance in her handbag. And that Millie could smell something quite alien to her!

Millie Goes to School

Soon Millie was quite the little celebrity in our local area, and she had many doggy friends on her travels. Whenever we came across children walking to school, one or two would come over to her.

"Millie is our favourite dog. She's so beautiful!" one girl said as she and her friend petted Millie.

Millie soaked up all those lovely little moments. One of our friends told us that Helen Ridge, the head teacher at Hempshill Vale School, had heard about a clever corgi that performed a little show of tricks and agility. She contacted us to ask if we would bring Millie to perform two shows for their Jubilee celebrations, one for the primary school and another one for the junior school.

We happily obliged, and Millie was more than willing. You could tell straight away that she was so confident with children around, and she just loved the school environment.

We'd taught Millie to go into a sleep position when we'd say, "Lie down. Look at you," just as we did when we dried her tummy off when she'd had a bath. But now, I added two extra commands of "Settle down" and "Go to sleep." It took a lot of time to get Millie to understand what we wanted her to do on just the command, "Sleep!"

And we taught her to jump up when she heard me call, "Wakey, wakey!" Millie started her show with the usual tricks, and the small children liked the one where she went to sleep on demand, rolling onto her back with one front paw in the air. I'd told the children that Millie would jump up from her sleep position only when she heard the "Wakey, wakey!" command. I said that I would give them a signal with my hand when they could shout it out. What made our little Millie even more impressive with this trick was that she closed her eyes at this command once she had laid down! I don't know to this day how she knew to do that, but she did! Then after being motionless for twenty seconds, I signalled the children, and they all shouted, "Wakey, wakey!" ten times louder than an adult! She jumped up and scampered about with everyone clapping and laughing. She did lots more tricks, and everyone, including the teachers loved it. It was an adoring audience. What more could Millie ask for?

At the end of the shows, Helen, the headmistress, was so pleased with the joy that Millie had brought to the school that she gave a contribution to Sense (and this was added to the money we raised and handed to the Hucknall branch).

Another of Millie's shows was for the Nuthall Friendship Club which held their meetings at the parish hall. Again, everything went so well it was as though we'd been doing it for years. Millie was a natural entertainer with her antics. At this show we'll always remember a gentleman who came up to us and told us it was in fact his ninetieth birthday.

"That was the best dog show I've seen in my entire life!" he said.

We thanked him. It was those kinds of comments at Millie's show that made all the hard work worthwhile.

Get Me to the Church on Time!

A week after we'd been to the Kimberley Age Concern at Kimberley Parish Hall we were performing at the Eastwood Baptist Church. That evening we duly arrived a little early and walked into the church to see if we could find out from someone who knew where they wanted us to perform. We didn't know a soul. People were looking at us very strangely as we were asking questions.

"I think you've come to the wrong church," someone finally said.

Apologies all around and we soon arrived at the proper place. We can laugh about it now, but it was a bit frantic at the time. We were so very busy, but Millie was having a ball.

Christmas came along and the little shows that Millie performed at Hucknall, Kimberley, Nuthall, and Eastwood were enhanced with a Christmas theme. In her summer shows one of her tricks was to find two cloths with Union Jack flags on the underside of both amongst about sixteen or so plain ones.

So, as it was Christmas, Elaine sewed a picture of Santa Claus on one and a picture of Rudolph on another. This trick was an adaptation of "Finding the scent cloth" test from training classes, and just like on test days, the cloths that we knew Millie would bring back were the ones that I had thoroughly rubbed through the palms of my hands an hour before. She was always quick to choose the ones that had more of Dad's scent on!

With "Jingle Bells" playing in the background, we turned the cloths face down on the floor. They vanished from sight as we gently threw down all the other white cloths.

"This is the snow falling, and Santa and Rudolph might have trouble finding their way out as they were covered with snow! Do you think Millie can help them?"

The children at the day centres loved this. When Millie came back into the room, the children all tried to tell Millie where Santa and Rudolph were. Some of the children couldn't be fooled! They hadn't taken their eyes off the ball at all! Sometimes I think that Millie was teasing them, because three or four times she would run over Santa and Rudolph and dip her nose over the correct cloths as she kept on running around them.

"He's there…he's there. He's there!"

The crescendo of small children shouting at the top of their voices rose to fever pitch before Millie found Santa and Rudolph! The little tease!

After the first show we did at Kettlebrook Lodge in Kimberley, we asked the playgroup staff if any of the children would like to stroke Millie. That provoked quite a stampede! We were surrounded by all those excited little ones. Each one of the children wanted to stroke and cuddle Millie, particularly her lovely big ears! One of the parents told us that they had a problem with their daughter when walking towards anyone with an animal on the footpath, but this was the first time she hadn't been afraid of a dog. We hoped that Millie had helped to pave the way for more peaceful encounters.

We created two new sketches for her Christmas

shows. The first saw us tell Millie to go to sleep and at the same time, we told the children that Millie always went to bed early on Christmas Eve. While she was sleeping, Elaine would play the famous line, “I’m dreaming of a White Christmas.” When they shouted, “Wakey, wakey!” Millie would run straight over to the Christmas tree at the other end of the hall and find her present, which was a feathered turkey toy! And she would bring it over for everyone to see. “Look what Santa’s left for me, under the Christmas tree!”

The second sketch was having Millie help with Christmas dinner which included her fetching a toy knife, fork, and a plate. She would then fetch the vegetables on demand. The final flourish was retrieving the rubbery, plucked turkey from the pot. We always placed that in the pot without anyone seeing it, so that it was a total surprise when her feathered turkey toy suddenly appeared plucked and cooked! That was such a laugh! She finished off tidying the kitchen up by placing the lids back onto the saucepans. She received plenty of praise and some turkey tit-bits for that (real turkey, of course!).

After a few run throughs of this sketch, I added something else into it. After she’d brought all the food back and placed it on the plate, everyone would be clapping.

“What a mess you’ve made, Millie! Aren’t you going to clean up?” I asked.

She would immediately run back to her cardboard cooker top and put the lids back onto the saucepans. She looked at me as if to say, “You only had to ask!” Thus followed a lot of praise and even louder applause! Magic moments again.

Into 2013 we went. Playing in the winter snow was soon behind us, and we’re back to getting all togged up for a walk over the fields every morning and evening, come rain or shine. Millie hardly ever cowed away from the bad weather.

"Well, are we going or not?" she asked with her eyes while she waited for us to get our wellies on.

We had an Easter show at the Wednesday Club in Nuthall. At the beginning I gave a talk about how we came up with the idea of Millie's variety act, the history of her training, and a little about her breed in general.

As it was Easter, we decided that we would number the balls that she fetched through the tunnels and jumps, and the corresponding raffle tickets would win an Easter egg. It all went brilliantly, and we received a lovely letter from the club's president saying that everyone loved the tricks Millie performed. She said that the following week some keys had been misplaced and everyone had said that Millie the corgi would easily find them if she'd been there!

Millie was getting quite a reputation—richly deserved, we thought. We had a call from the organizers of the Greasley Gathering at Newthorpe asking us to bring Millie to perform one of her special themed Coronation year shows. An exciting idea came to mind.

As it was sixty years since the Queen's Coronation, we thought we could have Millie run through the legs of sixty people at the show. Training commenced! After discussing this with Polly, she said that we could let Millie run through some of the other dog handler's legs. We tried eight people with legs astride to make a human tunnel like the one at agility class. I pointed and instructed Millie, "Through…through!" Millie loved it and made it look easy.

The Newthorpe show soon came around. We made the usual preparations early that morning and hung up the Coronation bunting kindly donated by Tesco in

Ilkeston. The bunting had Union Jacks, the Queen's Coronation crowns, and lots of pictures of corgis on it. More Union Jacks and flags were fastened onto the tunnels and jumps.

Halfway through the show we told everyone what we proposed to do. We needed twenty people to form a tunnel for one more trial run before we went outside to try for the big sixty tunnel. Some of our family attended which made it very special. The trial run went without a hitch, and before it was time to go outside, we did another variation on the "drug find."

The week before the show, we fastened two tea bags and a Brillo pad inside a cardboard box. We made small vent holes at the same position near the items so that Millie could get a good whiff of them. After a few trial runs with the whispered command, "Drugs," Millie went to the box, crouched down, and barked at it...every time!

So, at the show we placed a replica Coronation Crown into this special box and placed it amongst several other similar boxes. We asked someone to mix all the boxes up and space them apart. Elaine brought Millie back into the hall, and to the tune of "Land of Hope and Glory," she found the Queen's lost crown amongst all those boxes. (I don't know how she did it. Do you?)

"Okay! Let's go outside and do the tunnel run!" I said. Millie was accompanied out of the hall with her audience towards the tennis courts that were outside.

People of all ages gathered onto the tennis court. Twenty, thirty, forty. We soon had sixty people lined up ready for action.

"Are we all ready?" I asked. Millie was at the end of the tunnel with me, and Elaine went to the other end. "Millie, watch." Her eyes focused on me, waiting for the word of command. I paused, then pointed and shouted, "Through!"

Off she went! I began to run alongside her, but out she suddenly popped a third of the way down. *Oh, dear! What's happened?* All we could put it down to was that there might have been a small child in the way. *Never mind!* I asked everyone if they could make sure they had their legs as far apart as they could to give Millie a clear run.

After a few minutes, we were at the starting position again.

"Are we ready?" I asked again.

"Yes, we are!" everyone shouted back.

"Millie, watch," I said again. "Through!" I shouted.

Off she went. I ran alongside her again, and I was just about keeping up with her as she progressed down the tunnel of legs. "Through, Millie!" I shouted again, the excitement getting the better of me. And then suddenly I heard Elaine and Polly shout for Millie from the other end of the tunnel! I just couldn't keep up with her as she started to dash like a rabbit through a burrow.

Out she flew at the other end to rapturous applause. What a brilliant day that was. Millie was surrounded by so many friends, and every one of them seemed to enjoy the experience of something completely different. So much fun and raising money for a good cause—it couldn't get any better!

June came around quickly, and Mrs Jane Mainprize the headteacher at Awsworth Primary School heard about our corgi that performed these little shows and said that she was certain that everyone at the school would be delighted if she came. All her tricks went fine. The children particularly liked the one where I rubbed my nose and said, "I think I've got a cold coming on." Millie ran to the box of tissues strategically placed by

Elaine, picked out a tissue, and brought it back to me!

When we'd finished her show and were getting ready to leave, lots of children ran up to her in the playground wanting to give her lots more fuss. Did she like that? Of course she did! Millie never lost her puppy look, and children just loved her. And boy, did she love them!

Bluebells and Alarm Bells

Snowdrops, daffodils, and bluebells came and went in the local woods. Celandines and aconites, wood anemones, and the aroma of wild garlic abounded in the summer time. There's a lovely area in Watnall woods where some old school friends, Peter Charity and Geoff Walker, created a bench seat between two trees made from old wood. It's a wonderful resting place to watch the world go by, surrounded by nesting boxes they've fastened onto the trees and a feeding station opposite in the clearing. Nuthatches, robins, blue tits, chaffinches, and an occasional woodpecker. It was just the spot to drop a little water into Millie's travel dish and served as a meeting point for friends, canine and human alike!

Elaine and I loved to try to catch falling leaves in the woods. As I've said before Millie sometimes had a go at this, but she wasn't too good at it. We caught a few…and made a few wishes. She used to like doing what we called her moonwalk in the leaves. Several years ago, we saw her performing this sort of stationary kicking back similar to what dogs do to cover up their poo! I tidied up the path, told her she was a good girl, and gave her a tit-bit. Without another word from me, Millie began doing the moonwalk again.

"Look, Elaine, she's doing the moonwalk on demand."

It quickly became one of her party pieces. We'd just say, "Moonwalk, Mil," as we were walking onto the stage. Boy, that caused some delight and laughter.

Two dogs happened to come onto the scene about this time, with whom Millie struck a special friendship. Their names were Henry and Harry, a pair of cairn terriers who belonged to Kevin and Jan.

Henry and Harry were Millie's very special friends.

When we used to see them while we were walking over the fields in Watnall or in the woods, Millie would run full pelt towards them with her ears flapping all over the place. What a joy to see. All three dogs were such good friends. Oh! We mustn't miss out mentioning Gerry and Kim with Mac the terrier. Such a sweet little bloke, Mac was! He was virtually all white with the tips of his ears looking like they'd been dipped into a copper and chocolate mix. I could never resist giving those ears a special rub. Millie also had a special friendship with Mimi, a Yorkshire terrier, and her mum, Mary. We passed Mimi's house on our way to the woods on Trough Road. Millie always checked to see if Mimi was coming out for a walk by looking for that little nose going from side to side under the bottom of their garden gate. If so, it would be ears flapping time again! It's so good to remember these wonderful times.

***

Sometimes when we were settling down for the evening to watch something on the TV, Millie would look at us with her, "Aren't we going to have a play tonight?" Whatever we were interested in, how could we refuse? We would draw out her wicker box full of toys from behind the chair.

"What do you want to play with, then?"

Straight away she would dip her nose in and pull out what she wanted. Sometimes it was a pull rope, or "tuggy-tuggy" as Millie knew it. Sometimes it was her "corn on the cob man." All those silly toys they come up with! Just a little note here: Millie never ever destroyed her toys. Ever! That said, she would love it when we gave her an empty plastic milk bottle. Off she'd trot, chew the top off, and bring it to us. That was always worth a tiny treat, wasn't it? She was doing her bit of recycling! But destroy her toys…Never!

One of her much-loved toys was the hammer man. I would sit straight-legged on the carpet and put the little hammer man under my legs. She'd jump on top and scoot her nose down to the carpet to find the face of the thing. She really enjoyed the teasing and playing.

Then one night in July 2013, I said, "Okay, that's enough now, Millie. Let's settle down. Good girl. Let's give you a cuddle…Elaine!" I exclaimed. "Millie's got a lump under her neck!" We checked her over and concluded that she had an infection in one of her glands.

On the morning of the 10th July, 2013, we phoned the Lawrence Veterinary Practice in Eastwood to see if they could see her as soon as possible. We saw Ann, one of the vets whom Millie had a little soft spot for.

"Hello, Millie, let's have a look at you, shall we?" she said in her lovely Irish accent.

Ann drew some fluid from Millie's lymph gland to send off to a specialist. She told us that they would get the results in the next couple of days. It was an anxious wait.

Ann called to advise us to take Millie to a specialist veterinary hospital, The Willows at Solihull, due to some abnormalities they found. We set off early that morning with a lot of worries building up. Millie was oblivious! I think she thought she was going to the seaside!

It wasn't long before we were asked to take Millie into the consulting room to see James Elliot. He was very kind and re-assuring, and we immediately knew that she was going to receive the very best of care. After he examined Millie, he confirmed that she had Small Cell Lymphoma, and at this stage it would be better to leave it alone for six to eight weeks before treatment. He said that, as cancers go, this type of lymphoma was the better one to have because although it wasn't curable, it was controllable.

Life went on as normal apart from this dark cloud that followed us about. The weeks soon went by and it was soon time to go back to the Willows. We arrived a little earlier than necessary, so we took Millie for a walk in a nearby wooded area. We met someone that was exercising their dog and it turned out that he was going to the Willows too. He asked why Millie was here and after telling him, he revealed that his dog had the same problem and had been on treatment for three years. That certainly gave us hope.

We went into Willows and saw James Elliott again. He said that we should start Millie on a course of steroids and chemotherapy through tablets. We took his prescription and walked back to the car in something of a daze…

***

Amazingly, in just a month the swellings had shrunk and had virtually disappeared. We were so grateful to everyone concerned. At training sessions all our friends were wonderful and asked about Millie's health. She began to perk up, almost as if she had a new lease of life. We just couldn't believe how well she looked, running full pelt again up the hills that she knew so well. We seemed to forget about the lymphoma even though Elaine had to give Millie tablets every morning.

We were training one day, and I'd set up her jumps and her bowl of tennis balls. I told her to stay while I went to the other end of the hall. She looked so attentive and sweet, waiting for my call.

"She doesn't know that she's very poorly, does she?" I said to our friends that were seated around us.

I broke down, and well, I'm not ashamed one bit. I couldn't hold back my tears. Everyone was so kind and I quickly resumed Millie's exercise. Polly came over to me afterwards, and we had a chat. She said that it's so wonderful to have had the good fortune to look after and love a dog, but the most dreadful thing to lose them.

"You know, an animal is only lent to you," she said.

Her words helped to soften what we were going through and helped with the heartache.

Life went on, although we admit to spoiling Millie a *lot* more with extra trips to the seaside. She did love to swim and chase those elusive seagulls! She still skipped in the puddles, fit as a fiddle. We parked up on the seafront for fish and chips and treated Millie to lovely big chunks of fish. Well! Why not?

Doggie events came and went, and Millie won several rosettes for her tricks and obedience skills. We put the brakes on her show performances, but we still filled her time up as much as possible, and she *never* seemed to tire.

Millie's in Demand!

Before we knew it, Christmas was looming, and we received several phone calls asking if Millie could perform her little variety act. One of these was for the Eastwood Ladies Probus Club. On her little Christmas shows posters we wrote, "Come and have a very Millie Christmas!"

She performed with aplomb!

"Christmas Corgi Does Her Stuff," said the paper headline.

We took Millie to Kettlebrook Lodge in Kimberley for Millie's pre-school fans. I tended to watch the children during these shows—they were almost as entertaining as Millie! It was such a delight to see their faces and reactions, particularly to Millie finding the hidden Santa Claus and Rudolph cloths.

"He's there! He's there, Millie!"

But she was happily teasing them again! She ran back over the cloths with her nose down and scoop them up like one of the old Royal Mail trains that picked up the mail bags on the move! Brilliant! At the end of that show I asked if anyone wanted to stroke Millie as usual. Another stampede! We'll never forget being surrounded by these very happy children this Christmas. Wonderful!

2014 arrived faster than we could believe. Lovely, frosty mornings, walking through the fields all wrapped up in woolly scarves and gloves. Years before, we tried to put her in one of those special doggy weather coats. She glared at us with her "Millie unhappy" look.

"What are you doing?" Millie didn't want one of those silly coats. "I have my own coat, thank you very much!"

She didn't say that, of course, but she definitely meant it. Needless to say, we never tried to put another on her!

When she buried her nose in something of interest we would sometimes continue past her while we were chatting, but it wouldn't be too long before she would come thundering straight through the two of us like an express train with her breath puffing out of her like a steam engine in the cold air.

Another lovely character; Millie's friend, George.

Millie liked it when we crossed paths with Chris, Martin, and their lovely dachshund, Max. What a strong little character! He had several wars with his health and was a real battler! You could always tell he was so well loved by his mum and dad. Millie always loved to see George (and we enjoyed seeing his owner, Julie, a good friend of ours). He was a Schnoodle (Schnauzer Poodle cross). We first met George when Julie introduced him to Millie one morning when he was a pup. We talked about puppy training and told Julie we took Millie to Polly at the APT School for Dogs on Wednesdays. And our friendship just went from there! George was such a smart dog and always gave Millie a run for her money in little competitions on party days! Millie met up with George most weeks at training sessions and on walks.

Every walk was different, and there was always something new for her to experience and enjoy.

***

We got another request for Millie from Madeline, one of the organisers of the Greasley Gathering where she'd performed before. We went around May and organized the raffle using the numbered tennis balls as usual. We asked that all proceeds be donated to the Lymphoma and Haematology Unit at the Nottingham City Hospital. At this show we displayed Millie's rosettes and certificates from her training and competitions and photographs of her with children at schools and with folk at the care homes we'd visited. We included a couple of the Yours magazines with Millie's special feature. We were so proud of her as she sat for numerous photo shots in the hall. Yes, she had every right to be a little poser. It was another gem of a day.

Soon after this show we received a call from the

Spinney Day Centre. It was their fortieth anniversary and they wanted to celebrate with a special Millie attendance. Elaine's dad, Terry Fuller, had opened the centre when he was the Mayor of Broxtowe.

The day came, and everyone enjoyed the anniversary, which included a speech by the local county councillor, a visit by the Mayor of Broxtowe, and the cutting of a very special cake by the eldest resident there. Elaine's mum, Kathleen, went too, and she said it felt like five minutes since she'd attended the opening in 1975.

We hadn't prepared Millie for a performance, but one or two folks asked if it was possible to see Millie do any tricks or a little bit of dancing. Millie was all ears as if she knew exactly what they were asking for! Tables and chairs were soon moved, and off she went. Anything for a treat and a fuss! Someone came up to us and said that they'd heard of Millie, the clever corgi, and had missed her at the Greasley Gathering shows. They were so glad that they finally got a glimpse of her and said they couldn't wait to see a full performance in the future.

Millie Becomes an Olympian!

Winter arrived once more, and it soon got a little precarious under-foot so we started to go around the Basil Russell recreation ground. On one of these days we were there we came across a lady with a bulldog. He was lovely and very friendly, and she told us about how she took him into Haywood House, the City Hospital's hospice.

Stroking and loving dogs has been proven to be a relaxing therapy. We told her all about Millie, so she took our phone number and said that she would get in touch with Mrs Carol Maltby, the lady who organised events at the Hospice. Carol got in touch and we agreed to Millie doing a proper show with a Christmas theme.

We decided to start that show off with a bang! We brought in the stunt where Millie mimicked the hundred metre sprint she used to do at her shows when the Olympics were on. We put a strip of tape on the floor like a starting line and a fake Olympic torch at the other end of the room. Then I put her under starter's orders by making sure she was two metres away from the line.

"On your marks," I said in a low toned voice. Up she got near the line. "Get set." And with that instruction, she positioned herself like a pointer. I slowly raised my hand, shaping it to look like a starting pistol.

And then with a shout of "Bang!" from me.

She flew off faster than Usain Bolt, grabbed the Olympic torch, and brought it back to me. I put it straight into its holder (I made both of these especially for this event using half of a plastic bottle coloured gold from the inside, and I glued flames on the torch made from orange, red, and yellow crepe paper). After this, the Christmas Show would start. At least, that was the plan.

December arrived and we enjoyed frosty walks in the woods again. Millie seemed to like walking in the dark. Adventure again, running off and dancing in and out of the torch light.

"Come on, let's go home. We're cold even if you aren't," we shouted, and back she would bound to us.

Millie was showing us how she totally understood what we asked of her. If she was coming around the coffee table in the lounge, I'd only have to say, "Why don't you go around the other way, Mil?" and she'd immediately change direction. All in all, she loved her family life, and gosh, we loved her with all our worth!

Millie taking a well-earned break with her faithful bed companion.

One morning after she'd ravaged the plastic milk bottle and brought the red top back to me as she usually did, I said to her, "Come on then, Millie. We're off to the vets for your check-up."

We hadn't waited long before the vet's door opened.

"Millie Morley, please. Oh, there you are!" said Ann, one of Millie's regular vets.

She asked us to put Millie on the examination table. Millie had total trust in Ann and let herself be examined with hardly any fuss. Ann went through the stages of checking her teeth, (we always cleaned her teeth regularly—we think she loved the taste of doggy toothpaste), eyes, joints, and temperature.

"We often brush Millie's teeth at her children's shows to encourage them to brush theirs," I said. Ann had always loved to hear what Millie got up to in her performances.

"Sorry for interrupting, but I've got to tell you that Millie has a small lump in her tummy which I'm not happy with. I think it needs further investigation."

Immediately everything was thrown up into the air once again. I could tell that Ann was upset too but being her professional self, she quickly arranged for Millie to be seen at the Willows in Solihull the following day.

The next morning we went straight in to see James Elliott again. He said that they were going to carry out some tests and that we could pick Millie up about two p.m. We picked her up with heavy hearts and went home to await the results.

The very next day, James called. "I'm afraid Millie has soft cell sarcoma on her spleen."

He advised us that if he operated on Millie to remove the tumour it might be successful because dogs can survive without their spleen if necessary. But he couldn't give us any guarantees. We took his advice and booked Millie in for another operation on the 7th January, 2015. Meanwhile, we tried to continue as if everything were normal in the hope that she wouldn't pick up that there something was seriously wrong.

Only we knew, and we wanted to keep it that way. She was still running around in the woods, meeting all her friends, ears flapping about when she met Henry and Harry. Looking at her, our friends all found it hard to believe that she had this awful cancer problem. How on earth could she be so unlucky to get two types of cancer?

Millie Rocks Haywood House

Decisions had to be made. We had the Christmas show coming up at Haywood House at the City Hospital. What were we to do? Was Millie well enough? She certainly looked up for it; she was still flying into the kitchen after chasing pigeons on the lawn, looking mighty pleased with herself.

We didn't cancel her show, so in the week running up to it, we pinned a little poster on the noticeboard at the reception: "The Christmas Corgi Show with Millie Morley the Clever Corgi! Performing HERE on Saturday!" We hoped that it would give the patients' friends and family the opportunity to be there to watch Millie's performance together.

The show went incredibly well, and the nursing staff even managed to get the occasional glimpse. She started the show off with her Olympic Sprint too. Millie performed everything to a T. Best of all, she knew it too! She was full of herself throughout the show, jumping over the snowdrifts and generally having lots of fun. Her version of helping with Christmas dinner went brilliantly, and she was even joined by Santa Claus halfway through (the organizers of the show had arranged for this to happen and everything gelled together into a fun time). Everyone said how much they enjoyed seeing Millie...even Santa!

Her snowball raffle raised a good amount for the Lymphoma and Haematology Unit at the hospital. I think we can say that this show was one of the most satisfying we had ever done with Millie. If only you were there.

***

A few days after the Haywood House show, we had a phone call from Notts TV. I thought it was someone we knew having us on, but no, it was definitely a chap from their studio. He'd heard about Millie performing at the City Hospital and wanted us to bring her to the television studios on Christmas Eve at 6.15 p.m. to show everyone watching how she helped with a Christmas dinner. I wasn't sure, and I always discussed everything with Elaine who wasn't there, so I said that I would call him back.

I knew that we'd be busy on Christmas Eve like most people, so adding in a Millie show would be a struggle. However, given that it was only an hour or so of our time, we thought, why not? We wanted to give some fun on Christmas Eve to the children watching.

"Book us in. We'll be there!"

We readied Millie's props for the show, and the preparations seemed to take our minds off Millie's operation in the New Year. But after a drizzly walk on the 23rd December, I was drying Millie off and came across something that stopped me in my tracks. My goodness! I couldn't believe the lump in Millie's tummy had grown considerably in a matter of days.

I looked Millie in the eyes and said softly, "You're not going anywhere at Christmas, Millie."

We were upset of course, and I let Notts TV know that we'd be unable to bring Millie into Nottingham to do her show. Half an hour later the phone rang. It was James from the Willows calling to make sure that we were still bringing Millie in on the 7th of January (a month after her diagnosis). He didn't want Millie to suffer from a ruptured spleen if the tumour became too enlarged.

Over Christmas we were as careful as we could be. Millie didn't show any signs of being ill. The letter box noise, people coming to visit, before we could stop her, she would jump straight from her perch on the settee over one of the arms as though she were a spring chicken.

The 7th of January finally arrived after a subdued Christmas so off we went to the Willows. They operated, and we went to pick Millie up. Bless her! As soon as she saw us, she came half-running to us in the reception area with a big dressing and sticky plaster under her tummy with a lot of fur shaved away. The surgeon told us that he'd also removed a small lump from the outer wall of her tummy.

Now it was fingers, toes, and everything else crossed that we had stopped it. When we got home, she carefully came up to the small ramp we'd constructed (from the see-saw I had made that she used in her agility training) and got her used to coming in the back door without jumping in over the step. We'd got her using the ramp to protect her tum after her operation.

We managed to get out for a walk a week or so later, and we tried out her skid underbelly protector—she wasn't entirely happy about it but didn't try to gnaw it off! And it did its job to protect her.

A couple of visits to our local vets showed that Millie was recovering well and healing fine. She continued to take the same medication that she had for lymphoma.

January soon went. Millie started to go training again, and needless to say, she was being spoilt even more, especially by Polly. When I thought I had her under control, she would suddenly fly off to Polly at the other end of the hall. Special tit-bits given out by the trainer, including a fuss, wasn't the done thing, but so what? Millie was enjoying herself amongst friends.

Good-bye, Little Friend

On the 27th of January we went back to Lawrence's again as we thought Millie's tummy was a little swollen. Ann advised us to take her to Willows again to be checked over. We saw James Elliott again in early March, and we agreed that it would probably be better for her to have another operation to take a look at what was going on. Rightly or wrongly that's what we decided.

The news wasn't good. The cancer was a very aggressive type and had spread into her liver and other organs. We were given two choices; Millie could go on a course of chemotherapy injections (which they were unable to say whether that would make her more ill) or we could let the disease run its course without interfering. Even if the chemotherapy did help, James said that it might only double the small amount of time that Millie had left.

We went away to think about it for a couple of weeks. On further consultation with James, we decided to let Millie deal with this in the natural way and not to fill her full of chemicals.

Over the next few weeks we saw her begin to struggle. She would wander and roam around the garden haphazardly. She would stop and slowly walk to places in the garden where she didn't normally go as if she was looking for something but didn't know what. It was very upsetting to see her so puzzled. She would lay in the hall looking into one of the rooms for ages, whereas before, she would stare out of the French windows onto the garden. We could tell that she didn't feel at all happy and must have been feeling very ill.

We tried to be as normal as possible and make her as comfortable as possible. One day, we had a steady walk to the field up from Trough Lane in Watnall. We took her lead off and slowly went to the top. We arrived at the spot where she'd first had a glimpse of the big wide world as a puppy. She stopped in between the two trees at the top of the hill. After she sat down there, we stayed for quite a while looking over Nottingham.

"You've always liked it up here, haven't you?" I said, tears pooling in my eyes. We wandered back home through the Spinney where she used to play hide and seek with the family and remember the times she'd give the game away every time by barking where the children had hidden.

"That's not fair!" the grandchildren would shout.

The following day, on the 1st April, Millie didn't want her breakfast and that was very unusual. We rang the vets, and Ann said to bring her in. She thought it may be a good thing to try her on a diet that would be a little more palatable for her. She also recommended a course of Metacam, which she'd taken for an aching joint in the past, as she seemed to have developed a slight limp.

***

At teatime she only had a little of her new special food. She smelled it and gave it a lick, but that was it. She took herself off to bed quite early that night.

Early the following morning, Elaine said that she could hear Millie being sick in the kitchen. We went to her straight away. Bless her, she was so poorly. She had wet on the kitchen floor near the door and had been sick. We could see she didn't like that at all as she was always such a clean dog. Elaine and I crouched down together, and we both held her.

Elaine looked at me. "You know what we have to do today, don't you?" she said as her voice shook and tears tracked down her cheeks.

I nodded. We were both so upset as we cuddled Millie.

We rang the vets and spoke to Ann. We said that Millie had been very sick, and she seemed to be confused. After we told her what sort of state she was in, Ann advised us that we should do what we'd dreaded we had to do. We took Millie in at 9.45 a.m. Ann and everyone at Lawrence's were so kind. They knew what we were going through. This was the time that every loving owner of any animal dreads; the decision to end the life of such a wonderful friend. We looked into her beautiful, trusting eyes and told her she was always a good girl and how much we loved her. Cancer was being so cruel to her, and we couldn't let that go on.

Her flame of life was turned down gently and without any pain or stress, she fell asleep.

We had to be strong for her at the end. We'd been so fortunate to have been looking after this wonderful doggy all these years, and we've been told by many that she probably had more out of her life than most dogs that live longer than her. And yes, we like to think she did.

Millie gave a lot of joy to people of all ages in so many places and helped with several charities. Cancer is a terrible thing. At least we gave her a chance of a fight back, helping a little in the funds at the Lymphoma and Haematology Unit at the City Hospital.

It's now been over four years since we lost Millie.

We "borrowed" her for eight and a half wonderful, amazing, and action-packed years, but we still feel like we had to give her back early.

Reflections

Every now and then we get small reminders of the good times we all had with her. Just the other day, we heard Bobby Vee singing, "Rubber ball, I come bouncin' back to you," on Smooth Radio. When we were going out one morning, I saw a clothes peg on the lawn. When Millie was around, there was never a peg on the lawn or it would promptly be brought back to us for a treat reward! We were lucky to have so many magic moments that we'll never forget. We will always remember our little Millie being "Poetry in Motion."

I've found that writing Millie's story has been a great comfort, though it was hard to finish it when she was no longer with us. Her spirit and her memories will certainly live on for a long, long time.

Thank you, Millie, for sharing your life with us. You gave us all such a wonderful time. Bless your memory.

And thank you, the reader, for coming on this journey with us and our beautiful Millie Morley, the Welsh corgi. Remember to make a diary of all those special times that you have with your pet, so that you too will remember those magic moments you all shared… they'll be your "One in a Million."

What's Your Story?

Global Wordsmiths, CIC, provides an all-encompassing service for all writers, ranging from basic proofreading and cover design to development editing, typesetting, and eBook services. A major part of our work is charity and community focused, delivering writing projects to under-served and under-represented groups across Nottinghamshire, giving voice to the voiceless and visibility to the unseen.

To learn more about what we offer, visit: www.globalwords.co.uk

Other books by Global Words Press:

Desire, Love, Identity: From the Nottinghamshire LGBTQ Community
Aventuras en México: Farmilo Primary School
Life's Whispers: Journeys to the Hospice
Our World, The Things We Love: Awsworth Primary & Nursery School
Defining Moments: Stories from a Place of Recovery
World At War: Farmilo Primary School
Women's Stories, Women's Voices
The Victorian Vale: Farmilo Primary, Year Six
Times Past: Young at Heart
In Different Shoes: Stories of Trans Lives
Patriotic Voices: Stories of Service
From Surviving to Thriving: Reclaiming Our Voices
Fractured Voices: Breaking the Silence
Don't Look Back, You're Not Going That Way
Peace by Piece
Speaking OUT: LGBTQ Youth Memoirs
Late OutBursts: LGBTQ Memoirs